Fables & Folklore
READER'S THEATER
DEVELOP READING FLUENCY AND TEXT COMPREHENSION SKILLS

Written by
Dr. Margaret Allen, Ph.D.

Editor: Alaska Hults
Illustrator: Corbin Hillam
Cover Illustrator: Amy Vangsgard
Designer: Jane Wong-Saunders
Cover Designer: Barbara Peterson
Art Director: Tom Cochrane
Project Director: Carolea Williams

Table of Contents

6 = total number of parts

INTRODUCTION

Fluency instruction provides a bridge between being able to "read" a text and being able to understand it. Readers who decode word by word sound plodding and choppy. They are too busy figuring out the words to think about what they are reading. Fluent readers are accurate, quick, and able to read with expression. They make the reading sound interesting. Beyond the experience of the listener, fluent readers are also demonstrating skills that are crucial to their understanding of what they read. Fluent readers recognize words at a glance, group words into meaningful phrases, and move beyond the struggle to decode individual words. They are able to focus on making sense of what they read.

Reader's Theater is an exciting way to help children improve reading fluency without being too time intensive for the teacher. It requires no props and no additional teaching skills on your part, and it is not difficult to manage. Reader's Theater promotes better reading comprehension because children who have learned to read a passage expressively also come to better understand its meaning. In addition, research says that these gains transfer well to new text. Reader's Theater also addresses standards in listening while providing a fun environment for everyone involved. When children practice their lines, they read and reread the same passages. Under your direction, they gradually add more expression, read more smoothly, and find any subtle meanings in the passages.

The scripts in *Fables & Folklore Reader's Theater* are designed for fluency instruction. The overall purpose is to provide children with text at their reading level that is fun to read. The scripts in this collection serve another useful purpose— they introduce children to stories originally passed along in the oral tradition. Fables, folktales, and tall tales are part of our history. However, many children may be unfamiliar with them, and, as they get

older, often miss allusions to them in more complex literature. Use these scripts to fill that literary void and to introduce children to stories enjoyed by their ancestors. In addition, all the scripts provide the following hallmarks of a good Reader's Theater text:

• fast-moving dialogue
• action
• humor
• narrative parts

The scripts in *Fables & Folklore Reader's Theater* are intended to be read in groups of 5 to 8 children. Each script is prefaced by information that helps you direct child learning and is preceded by reproducibles that support extended learning and reading comprehension.

HOW TO USE THIS BOOK

Each Reader's Theater script should be covered over the course of five practice days (although those days do not need to be consecutive). The first day should include some or all of the elements of the suggested reading instruction. It should also include an expressive reading by you of the script as children read along silently. On each of the following days, give children an opportunity to practice their reading. On the final day, have each group read its script for the class.

Four sections that support reading instruction precede each script:

- **Script Summary** provides a plot summary for the script.

- **Reading Rehearsal** features detailed notes for fluency instruction.

- A brief description of each **Part** introduces children to the characters. (See page 5 for more information.)

- The **Drama Coach's Corner** provides comprehension activities, suggestions for discussion of the story of the script, and directions for the accompanying reproducibles.

On the first day of instruction, use the background and information about each character to tell children what the script will be about and describe the characters.

Read aloud the script, modeling clear enunciation and a storyteller's voice. Do not be afraid to exaggerate your expression—it will hold the attention of your audience and stick more firmly in their minds when they attempt to mimic you later. Model the pacing you expect from them as they read.

Finish the reading instruction by discussing the fluency tips with children and having them complete any activity described in this section.

Now it is time to give children a copy of the script! Use the following schedule of child practice for a five-day instruction period.

Day 1	After following the steps outlined on page 4, give each child a personal copy of the script. Have children place the script in a file folder, and help them staple the pages in place. Invite them to decorate the cover of the file folder. Read aloud the script together as a class, in small groups, or in pairs.
Days 2 and 3	Assign children to a group. Have children gather to read aloud the script as many times as time permits. Have them change roles with each reading. Move from group to group, providing feedback and additional modeling as needed. At the *end* of day 3, assign roles or have children agree on a role to own.

Day 4	Have each group read aloud the script. Move from group to group and provide feedback. Have children discuss their favorite lines at the end of each reading and why the manner in which they are read works well. Repeat. Encourage children to check out a script for practice at home. Have children make placards from tagboard to identify their character.
Day 5	Have each group perform its script for the rest of the class (or other audience members provided by buddy classes and/or school personnel).

Throughout the week, or as time permits, provide children with the comprehension activities described in the Drama Coach's Corner. These are optional and do not have to be completed to provide fluency instruction; however, many provide children with additional background information that may help them better understand the characters or setting of the script.

Additional Tips

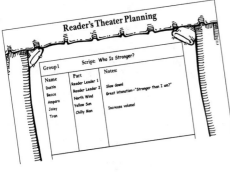

- Use the Reader's Theater Planning reproducible (page 6) to track the assigned roles for each group and to jot down any informal observations you make for assessment. Use these observations to drive future fluency instruction.

- Notice that there are no staging directions in the scripts. These plays are written to be read expressively in a storyteller's voice. If the focus is placed on *acting out* the script, children will shift their focus from the reading to the movement. If children become enchanted with a script and want to act it out, invite them to do so after they have mastered the reading. Then, have the group go through the script and brainstorm their own staging directions. Props should not be included until all fluency goals have been met.

- To fit fluency instruction into an already full day of instruction, it will work best to have all groups work on the same script. This will permit you to complete the first day's activities as a whole class. Children will enjoy hearing how another child reads the same lines, and some mild competition to read expressively will only foster additional effort.

- The roles with the greatest and least number of words to read are noted in the Parts section. The ⬆ and ⬇ indicate a higher or lower *word count*. They are not a reflection of reading level. The Reader Leader parts usually reflect the highest reading level. However, less fluent readers may benefit from having fewer words to master. More advanced readers may benefit from the challenge of the greater word count.

- **First-Grade Teachers:** For the first few months of the year, you may wish to try poems and songs as choral reading in parts to prepare children for independent reading of roles in Reader's Theater.

- **Second-Grade Teachers:** Your children may not need all of the scaffolding presented in the Reading Rehearsal section. Present only what you deem necessary, and move on to the next section.

- Any part can be read in unison. Encourage less fluent readers to pair with more fluent readers for choral reading of a part.

Reader's Theater Planning

Group 1   Script: _____

Name	Part	Notes:

Group 2   Script: _____

Name	Part	Notes:

Group 3   Script: _____

Name	Part	Notes:

Fables & Folklore Reader's Theater © 2004 Creative Teaching Press

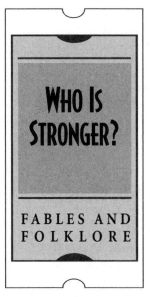

WHO IS STRONGER?

FABLES AND FOLKLORE

SCRIPT SUMMARY

Who Is Stronger? is based on Aesop's fable The North Wind and the Sun. The moral of this fable is, "Gentleness and kind persuasion win where force and bluster fail." Another fable connection is the saying, "You catch more flies with honey than with vinegar." Set the stage for this contest between gentleness and force by using classroom scenarios to lead a discussion about problem solving. Ask if kind words and discussion should prevail over hitting or angry responses. Ask when strong words are appropriate.

READING REHEARSAL

When you read aloud the script for children, have them listen for the following:

- Demonstrate bravado by increasing modulation and emphasizing *I* and any words that communicate achievement. Have children mimic you. For example, you would read **North Wind:** *I am SO strong!*

- Notice the exclamation points during the argument about who is stronger. How should children's voices sound during the argument?

- Call attention to the words that represent sounds, such as **North Wind:** *Whoosh! Whoosh!* Read them, elongating the words (e.g., Whooosh!). Have children copy you.

- On the last page of the script, North Wind's voice should sound very different—he lost and is dejected. His voice is now quieter and he shows less bravado.

Read the whole script again with the class divided into the two main roles and you reading the rest of the text. Notice which children read fluently using the tips they just practiced. If they do not seem ready to read independently in roles, review the whole process before assigning roles.

PARTS

Reader Leader 1
Reader Leader 2
North Wind
Yellow Sun
Chilly Man

DRAMA COACH'S CORNER

Kind Words, Strong Words

OBJECTIVE
Use character empathy to discuss when kind words and strong words are appropriate.

ACTIVITY

Give each child a **Kind Words or Strong Words? reproducible (page 9).** Discuss times when kind words or gentleness is preferred and times when strong words or force is needed. Encourage children to talk about their responses. You may use the third example to teach children about stranger safety, such as having a password that only the parent knows (to foil a stranger who claims the parent sent him or her to pick up the child). Use your judgment based on the maturity level of your children.

Literature Response

OBJECTIVE
Recall and respond to a scene from the story.

ACTIVITY

Give each child a **Who Is Stronger? reproducible (page 10).** Have children illustrate a scene from the story and write or dictate on **lined paper** a sentence about why they chose that scene to illustrate.

Name_____   Date _____

Kind Words or Strong Words?

PLEASE!   NO!

Directions: Read each example. Think about what happened. Then write how you would respond. Find a partner and talk about your responses.

What Happened?	Kind Words	Strong Words
Your friend uses your red crayon without asking first.		
What Happened?	**Kind Words**	**Strong Words**
You see your friend picking on another friend. It makes you mad.		
What Happened?	**Kind Words**	**Strong Words**
A stranger tells you to get in the car.		
What Happened?	**Kind Words**	**Strong Words**
Your friend talks to you during class. You do not want to get in trouble. At recess, you talk to your friend.		

Fables & Folklore Reader's Theater © 2004 Creative Teaching Press

Name_____   Date _____

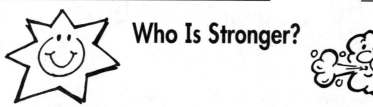

Who Is Stronger?

Directions: Think about the story. Draw a picture of your favorite part of the story. Tell why you like that part of the story.

WHO IS STRONGER?

Retold and adapted by Margaret Allen

PARTS

Reader Leader 1
Reader Leader 2
North Wind
Yellow Sun
Chilly Man

Reader Leader 1: North Wind and Yellow Sun are friends.

Reader Leader 2: They both live in the sky.

Reader Leader 1: North Wind is very strong.

Reader Leader 2: Yellow Sun is very strong.

North Wind: I am SO strong!

Reader Leader 1: . . . brags North Wind.

Yellow Sun: I am SO strong, too!

Reader Leader 2: . . . answers Yellow Sun.

North Wind: You, Yellow Sun—strong? I think not!

Yellow Sun: I am stronger than you are, North Wind.

North Wind: Stronger than I am? You must be joking, Yellow Sun!

Yellow Sun: I am not joking, North Wind. I am stronger than you are!

Fables & Folklore Reader's Theater © 2004 Creative Teaching Press

WHO IS STRONGER?

North Wind: You are not!

Yellow Sun: I am, too!

Reader Leader 1: This goes on and on for days.

Reader Leader 2: Finally, the North Wind says . . .

North Wind: I can prove I am stronger.

Yellow Sun: How?

North Wind: Do you see Chilly Man? He is down the road.

Yellow Sun: Yes, I see Chilly Man. He has his coat on.

North Wind: That's right.

Yellow Sun: How can Chilly Man help us? How can he know who is stronger?

North Wind: Let us try to make him take off his coat.

Yellow Sun: What? Take off his coat?

North Wind: That's right. The first one of us who makes Chilly Man take off his coat is stronger. Is it a deal?

Yellow Sun: Yes, it is a deal. You go first.

Fables & Folklore Reader's Theater © 2004 Creative Teaching Press

WHO IS STRONGER?

Reader Leader 1: Yellow Sun hides behind a cloud.

Reader Leader 2: North Wind blows.

North Wind: Whoosh! Whoosh!

Chilly Man: I am glad I have my coat. This wind is very cold!

Reader Leader 1: North Wind whistles.

North Wind: Whew! Whew!

Chilly Man: Listen to that wind. It makes me colder.

Reader Leader 2: North Wind blows and blows and blows!

Chilly Man: I am SO glad I have my coat!

Reader Leader 1: And with that, Chilly Man holds on to his coat.

Reader Leader 2: Out pops Yellow Sun.

Yellow Sun: It is my turn now.

Reader Leader 1: Yellow Sun comes out from behind the cloud.

Reader Leader 2: Yellow Sun shines gently.

Yellow Sun: Ssssss.

Chilly Man: I am getting warm.

Fables & Folklore Reader's Theater © 2004 Creative Teaching Press

WHO IS STRONGER?

Reader Leader 1: Chilly Man lets his coat go.

Reader Leader 2: He does not hold it tightly now.

Reader Leader 1: Then Yellow Sun shines warmer.

Yellow Sun: Sssssss!

Chilly Man: I am getting very warm.

Reader Leader 2: Chilly Man unbuttons his coat.

Reader Leader 1: Then Yellow Sun becomes hot.

Yellow Sun: SSSSSSSSSSSSS!

Chilly Man: Oh, my! I am *very* hot. I must sit under this tree and cool off!

Reader Leader 2: And with that, Chilly Man takes off his coat. He puts it on the grass. Then he sits down to cool off.

Yellow Sun: See, North Wind? I *am* stronger than you are!

North Wind: Yes, you made him take off his coat. You win.

Reader Leader 1: . . . says North Wind in a sad voice.

Fables & Folklore Reader's Theater © 2004 Creative Teaching Press

WHO IS STRONGER?

North Wind: You win. But how? I blew and blew. I blew and roared and whistled. I was sure I was stronger. How did *you* win?

Yellow Sun: I was gentle. You were very harsh. You made him hold tight.

Reader Leader 2: Yes, Yellow Sun won. She proved she was stronger.

Reader Leader 1: Yellow Sun did with gentleness . . .

Reader Leader 2: . . . what North Wind could not do by force!

FIDDLE-DIDDLE!

FABLES AND FOLKLORE

SCRIPT SUMMARY

Fiddle-Diddle! is based on Aesop's fable The Ants and the Grasshopper. The moral of this fable is, "There's a time for work and a time for play." This moral inspired the saying, "Quit fiddling around!" Connect this common saying to the fable for children. Set the stage by leading a discussion on work time and play time. Encourage children to provide examples of each and consequences when play is substituted for work! Record children's responses on chart paper for future reference.

READING REHEARSAL

Copy the script onto overhead transparencies, and display them. Write the worker ants' and Grasshopper's repeating lines from the script on chart paper, and display it. Read the script. Then, reread it but pause to have children read the repeating lines from the chart. Have them listen for the following:

• The ants' line has a serious tone and Grasshopper's is more playful.

• The Queen Ant will probably speak slowly and enunciate very clearly. Read the part with an almost marching pace, and speak each word crisply. Then, have children repeat after you.

Divide the class into three groups, one to read the worker ants' rhyme, one to read Grasshopper's rhyme, and a third to read Queen Ant's part.

PARTS

Reader Leader 1
Reader Leader 2
Reader Leader 3
⬛ Grasshopper

⬛ Queen Ant
Worker Ant 1
Worker Ant 2
Worker Ant 3

DRAMA COACH'S CORNER

Work and Play

OBJECTIVE

Relate theme of story to children's own experience.

ACTIVITY

Give each child a **Time for Work, Time for Play reproducible (page 18).** Have children reflect on, discuss, and write about work time and play time. Invite children to share their responses.

Write a New Ending

OBJECTIVE

Invent a new ending.

ACTIVITY

Give each child a **Sharing with Grasshopper reproducible (page 19).** Discuss with children the script's ending. Have them consider how the story might have ended differently. Ask *Would the new endings make sense? Why or why not?* Then, have children write about or draw pictures that depict a different ending—one in which Queen Ant shares the ants' food. Invite children to tell which ending they prefer.

Name_____   Date _____

Time for Work, Time for Play

Directions: Read the title of each box. Draw or write about your work time and play time at home and at school.

Work Time at School	Play Time at School
Work Time at Home	**Play Time at Home**

Fables & Folklore Reader's Theater © 2004 Creative Teaching Press

Sharing with Grasshopper

Directions: Think about the story "Fiddle-Diddle!" Give the story a new ending. Draw or write about an ending in which Queen Ant shared the ants' food with Grasshopper.

FIDDLE-DIDDLE!
Retold and adapted by Margaret Allen

PARTS

Reader Leader 1
Reader Leader 2
Reader Leader 3
Grasshopper
Queen Ant
Worker Ant 1
Worker Ant 2
Worker Ant 3

Reader Leader 1: It was almost summer.

Reader Leader 2: And you know what that means?

Reader Leader 3: Yes, work time. Time to store up food for winter.

Reader Leader 1: Queen Ant called her workers.

Queen Ant: My workers, draw near. It is time. Work time is here.

Reader Leader 2: The worker ants stopped playing. They stopped to listen to their queen.

Queen Ant: It is time to gather food. The sun is hot in the sky. We must store food now or when winter comes, we die.

Worker Ant 1: Did you hear that? Work time.

Worker Ant 2: So soon?

Worker Ant 3: No time for play now.

Reader Leader 3: And the worker ants started to work.

Reader Leader 1: Along came Grasshopper. He had his fiddle.

Fables & Folklore Reader's Theater © 2004 Creative Teaching Press

Reader Leader 2: He was playing and dancing.

Reader Leader 3: Grasshopper danced on until he met the first worker ant.

Grasshopper: Hi! Want to play? Want to play with me today?

Worker Ant 1: Oh, Grasshopper. No time for play. Not today! You must store food. Time is little. Time is little. Do not fiddle!

Grasshopper: I will store food someday, I know. But not today. On with the show! Fiddle-diddle. Fiddle-riddle-diddle. I am Grasshopper. Born to fiddle.

Reader Leader 1: Grasshopper danced on until he met the second worker ant.

Grasshopper: Hi! Want to play? Want to play with me today?

Worker Ant 2: Oh, Grasshopper. No time for play. Not today! You must store food. Time is little. Time is little. Do not fiddle!

Grasshopper: I will store food someday, I know. But not today. On with the show! Fiddle-diddle. Fiddle-riddle-diddle. I am Grasshopper. Born to fiddle.

Reader Leader 2: Grasshopper danced on until he met the third worker ant.

Grasshopper: Hi! Want to play? Want to play with me today?

Worker Ant 3: Oh, Grasshopper. No time for play. Not today! You must store food. Time is little. Time is little. Do not fiddle!

Grasshopper: I will store food someday, I know. But not today. On with the show! Fiddle-diddle. Fiddle-riddle-diddle. I am Grasshopper. Born to fiddle.

Reader Leader 3: Grasshopper danced and played. Grasshopper played and danced.

Reader Leader 1: And the worker ants worked. They worked and worked.

Reader Leader 2: They had stored a lot of food.

Reader Leader 3: The sun was not so hot in the sky. The wind was turning cold.

Queen Ant: My workers, draw near. Thank you for your work. Winter time is here.

Reader Leader 1: The worker ants stopped working.

Reader Leader 2: They stopped to listen to their queen.

Fables & Folklore Reader's Theater © 2004 Creative Teaching Press

Queen Ant: You worked to gather food when the sun was hot in the sky. We stored up lots of food. Now winter's here. We will not die.

Reader Leader 3: Just then, Grasshopper, shivering in the cold, danced up to the queen.

Grasshopper: Oh, Queen Ant. I'm so glad I danced by. Please let me share your food. There is no food in this winter sky.

Queen Ant: Who comes to me today? Who is it? Please say.

Grasshopper: Oh, great queen. Fiddle-diddle. Diddle-fi. It's me, Grasshopper. Please give me food. Or I will die.

Queen Ant: I am sorry, Grasshopper. I'm sorry you danced by today.

Grasshopper: Sorry?

Queen Ant: Yes! I'm sorry! I'm sorry when you could have worked, you only chose to play. We can't share our food with you. We can't! Not today!

Reader Leader 1: And with that, Queen Ant turned away.

Reader Leader 2: Grasshopper did not get food.

Reader Leader 3: No! No food from the ants today.

Reader Leader 1: And now he knew he should have worked . . .

Reader Leader 2: . . . when all he did was play!

Fables & Folklore Reader's Theater © 2004 Creative Teaching Press

LES LION
AND
MOE MOUSE

FABLES AND
FOLKLORE

SCRIPT SUMMARY

Les Lion and Moe Mouse is based on Aesop's fable The Lion and the Mouse. The moral of this fable is, "A kindness is never wasted." Set the stage for reading by asking children if they have ever helped their parents or someone else much bigger and/or older than they are. Allow time for children to share their personal stories. Then, ask if they think a little mouse could ever help a great big lion. Have them explain why or why not.

READING REHEARSAL

Copy the script onto overhead transparencies, and display them. When you read aloud the script for children, have them listen for the following:

- How might a mouse sound different from a lion? Reread the script, emphasizing the high voice of the mouse and the deep tones of the lion. Have children mimic your reading.

- How does someone sound when he or she doesn't believe you? Reread **Les Lion:** *How could little you help great big me?*

Read the script together as a class, with children reading all of Les Lion's parts.

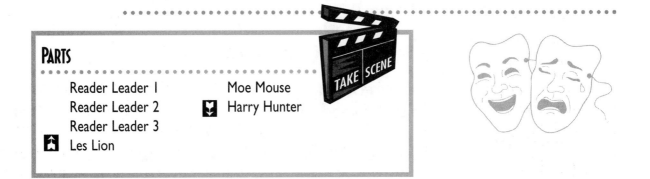

PARTS

Reader Leader 1
Reader Leader 2
Reader Leader 3
Les Lion

Moe Mouse
Harry Hunter

DRAMA COACH'S CORNER

Actions and Consequences

OBJECTIVE
Explore cause and effect in a story.

ACTIVITY

Give each child an **Actions and Consequences reproducible (page 26)**. Discuss with children the events of the story. Ask *What would have happened if Les Lion had eaten Moe Mouse?* Talk about actions and consequences. Point out that Les freed Moe, so Moe was able to free Les. Without Moe alive, the story would have a different ending. Have children complete the reproducible and share their work with the class.

Sequencing

OBJECTIVE
Retell the key events of a story.

ACTIVITY

Give each child **The Lion and the Mouse reproducible (page 27)**. Have children retell the story to demonstrate their comprehension of the story structure.

Actions and Consequences

Directions: Think about the story. What would have happened if Les Lion had not let Moe Mouse go. How would the story have ended? Draw or write about that ending.

Name_____   Date _____

The Lion and the Mouse

Directions: List details about the story in each box.
Find a partner and retell the story.

Characters:
First,
Next,
Then,
Last,

LES LION AND MOE MOUSE

Retold and adapted by Margaret Allen

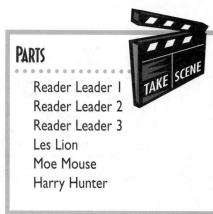

PARTS

Reader Leader 1
Reader Leader 2
Reader Leader 3
Les Lion
Moe Mouse
Harry Hunter

Les Lion: Yawn! Yawn! . . .

Reader Leader 1: . . . said Les Lion.

Les Lion: I am so sleepy. I need rest. I think I will take a nap in the woods.

Reader Leader 2: "Growl! Growl!" sounded Moe Mouse's stomach.

Moe Mouse: I am so hungry. I need food. I think I will take a walk and look for seeds.

Reader Leader 3: "Rustle, rustle!" It was Harry Hunter in the brush in the woods.

Harry Hunter: I am so late. I need a big cat for the zoo. I think I will go on a lion hunt.

Reader Leader 1: Les Lion went to sleep in the woods. He rested his head on his paws.

Fables & Folklore Reader's Theater © 2004 Creative Teaching Press

LES LION AND MOE MOUSE

Reader Leader 2: Moe Mouse went for a walk in the woods. She scratched for seeds to eat.

Reader Leader 3: Harry Hunter went on a hunt in the woods. He looked for a big cat to trap.

Reader Leader 1: "Snee-snore! Snee-snore!" Les was in a deep sleep.

Reader Leader 2: Moe Mouse walked, scratched, and ate. All of a sudden, she hit a bump.

Moe Mouse: Oh! What is this big bump in the road? It feels funny.

Reader Leader 3: And with that, Moe Mouse squeezed it as hard as she could. It was NOT a bump!

Les Lion: Hey, what are you doing to my nose, little mouse? Stop that! And stop that now!

Reader Leader 1: And with that, Les Lion let out a big roar.

Les Lion: ROAR!

Reader Leader 2: The sound scared Moe Mouse. She froze in her spot. She could not run away.

Moe Mouse: I am so sorry, great lion. I thought your nose was a bump on the road. I did not mean to hurt you!

Les Lion:	What? A little thing like you hurt a great big cat like me? I think not!
Reader Leader 3:	But Les took his paw and rubbed his nose anyway. Then he stuck out his other paw to trap Moe Mouse.
Les Lion:	I could hurt you now. I could take my paw and crush you!
Moe Mouse:	I know, great one. But please do not hurt me. Please spare me. I will pay you back someday.
Les Lion:	HA! HA! HA! *You* help *me*? How could little you help great big me?
Moe Mouse:	I'm not sure, great one. But I will. I will. I promise! I will help you someday.
Les Lion:	You are so funny. You make me laugh. Okay! I will let you go. Be off with you!
Reader Leader 1:	This time Moe Mouse was not frozen. This time she ran as fast as she could.
Reader Leader 2:	Les Lion lay down. He wanted to nap some more.

Fables & Folklore Reader's Theater © 2004 Creative Teaching Press

LES LION AND MOE MOUSE

Reader Leader 3: But Les did not know that Harry Hunter had heard the great roar. Harry knew a big cat was nearby.

Reader Leader 1: He came to the spot in the woods—the very spot— where Les was sleeping.

Harry Hunter: Just what I need—a big cat for the zoo. And a sleeping big cat—all the better!

Reader Leader 2: Harry got his big net ready.

Harry Hunter: Take this, big cat!

Reader Leader 3: He threw the net around Les Lion.

Harry Hunter: Yes! Now you are in my net. Now you are mine!

Reader Leader 1: Poor Les. He was sleeping soundly. He didn't hear Harry Hunter. He woke up to find himself trapped in the net.

Les Lion: H—E—L—P!!!!!!!!!!! H—E—L—P!!!!!!!!!!!

Reader Leader 2: Moe Mouse stopped running. She sat up and listened. The cry sounded like Les Lion—the great one who just this night had let her go.

LES LION AND MOE MOUSE

Reader Leader 3: Moe Mouse knew what she had to do. She had to help Les. She started running—toward Les this time.

Reader Leader 1: Harry Hunter had tied the lion with a rope. Then, happy with his catch, went to sleep in his tent.

Reader Leader 2: Now Moe Mouse could see Les Lion and the rope.

Moe Mouse: Oh, what can I do to help him? What? Oh, what?

Reader Leader 3: Just then, she knew what to do. She would chew on the rope and set Les free!

Les Lion: Who is there?

Moe Mouse: It is only me, great one, Moe Mouse. I am here to help you. I am here to set you free.

Reader Leader 1: And with that, Moe chewed and chewed and chewed and chewed. She was tired, but she did not stop.

Reader Leader 2: Finally, she chewed all the way through the rope.

Les Lion: I can pull free now. Move, little one.

Reader Leader 3: Les pulled and pulled. The rope broke. He was free.

Fables & Folklore Reader's Theater © 2004 Creative Teaching Press

LES LION AND MOE MOUSE

Les Lion: Thank you, little one. I didn't believe you before. But you did help me. You set me free. Thank you!

Moe Mouse: Yes! You laughed at me. But I did pay you back. I did! Now, let's go before that hunter hears us!

Reader Leader 1: And with that, the two were off, big and small, through the woods. Big and small, kindness for all!

Fables & Folklore Reader's Theater © 2004 Creative Teaching Press

CRYING WOLF

FABLES AND FOLKLORE

SCRIPT SUMMARY

Crying Wolf is based on Aesop's fable The Shepherd Boy and the Wolf. The moral of this fable is, "Liars are not believed even when they speak the truth." Set the stage by asking children to think about a time when someone told them a fib. The next time that person told them something, did they believe him or her? Talk about their responses. Introduce the words *shepherd, flock, village,* and *villagers.* Define them with examples. Talk about what "giving your word" means.

READING REHEARSAL

When you read aloud the script for children, have them listen for the following:

- Mr. Shepherd conveys trust to Will and the villagers by speaking calmly. He speaks slowly and does not raise his voice.

- Will is young and a little immature. He is not sure he is prepared to be responsible for the sheep. He may speak more quickly, almost running words together. Point out that the reader should not read *too* quickly or the audience will not be able to understand the lines. However, Will should speak more quickly than Mr. Shepherd.

Have half of the class read Mr. Shepherd's part and half read Will's role while you read the other parts.

PARTS

Reader Leader 1
Reader Leader 2
Reader Leader 3
★ Mr. Shepherd
★ Will Fibber
✦ The Villagers (up to three children)

DRAMA COACH'S CORNER

A Letter of Apology

> **OBJECTIVE**
> Investigate the character of Will Fibber.

ACTIVITY

Give each child a **Letter to Mr. Shepherd reproducible (page 36).** Discuss with children Will Fibber's role. Ask *What will Will tell Mr. Shepherd when he returns from his trip?* Invite the children to role-play Mr. Shepherd and Will's meeting. Have children pretend they are Will Fibber to complete the reproducible. Have volunteers share their letter to Mr. Shepherd with the class.

Flap Book

> **OBJECTIVE**
> Recall and respond to a scene from the story.

ACTIVITY

Give each child a **Flap Book reproducible (page 37)** and a **6" x 7¾" (15 cm x 19.5 cm) paper rectangle.** Have children draw a villager, Will, or Mr. Shepherd on the rectangle, glue it to the flap book, and write about the character on the bottom page.

Name_____

Letter to Mr. Shepherd

Directions: Pretend you are Will. Use this form to write an apology letter to Mr. Shepherd. Explain what happened. Tell how you feel.

Date _____

Dear Mr. Shepherd,

While you were away on your trip, _____

_____

_____

_____

_____

_____

_____

I feel _____

_____

Your shepherd,

Will Fibber

Fables & Folklore Reader's Theater © 2004 Creative Teaching Press

Name_____

Flap Book

Directions: Draw your character on the rectangle flap. Glue the left side of the flap on the dotted line. Write words to describe the character on this page.

CRYING WOLF
Retold and adapted by Margaret Allen

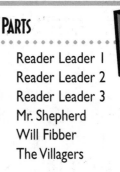

PARTS

Reader Leader 1
Reader Leader 2
Reader Leader 3
Mr. Shepherd
Will Fibber
The Villagers

Reader Leader 1: Will Fibber was a boy who watched sheep. He worked for Mr. Shepherd.

Reader Leader 2: Mr. Shepherd had a huge flock of sheep. He kept them in a field near the woods.

Reader Leader 3: Will Fibber had a sheep dog. Sheep to watch and a sheep dog. That was all Will Fibber had.

Reader Leader 1: It was morning. Mr. Shepherd went to Will Fibber's house to wake him.

Mr. Shepherd: Will Fibber, it is time to get up. It is time to go to work. Get up and go to the field. Watch the sheep. Watch them well.

Will Fibber: Okay, Mr. Shepherd. I will get up. I will go to the field. I will watch the sheep.

Mr. Shepherd: Good. But remember what I told you?

Will Fibber: About what?

Mr. Shepherd: About Sneaky Wolf, the gray wolf who lives in the woods!

Fables & Folklore Reader's Theater © 2004 Creative Teaching Press

CRYING WOLF

Will Fibber: Is Sneaky Wolf real? I think he is just a story.

Mr. Shepherd: Oh, no, Will Fibber. He is real. If you see Sneaky Wolf, run to the village.

Will Fibber: Why?

Mr. Shepherd: The villagers will help you. They will drive Sneaky Wolf away. They gave me their word.

Reader Leader 2: And with that, Mr. Shepherd left for a long trip.

Reader Leader 3: Will got up. He got dressed. He walked to the field.

Reader Leader 1: Will watched the sheep. Will played with the dog. Will watched the sheep some more.

Will Fibber: This is boring! It is very boring to watch sheep. All I have is this dog. All I have is this dog . . . and all of these sheep to watch. Boring!

Reader Leader 2: Will Fibber thought of a plan. He thought of a funny plan. He would trick the villagers.

Reader Leader 3: He would trick them. Then he would laugh at them. Then it would not be so boring.

Will Fibber: I will run into the village. Then I will call the villagers. I will tell them Sneaky Wolf is here. I will tell them Sneaky Wolf is stealing the sheep.

Fables & Folklore Reader's Theater © 2004 Creative Teaching Press

Reader Leader 1: Will left the sheep dog. He left the sheep. He ran all the way to the village.

Reader Leader 2: When he got to the village, he saw the villagers. He began to cry out.

Will Fibber: Help! I need help! Sneaky Wolf is in the field. Sneaky Wolf is stealing the sheep. Help me now!

The Villagers: Do not worry, Will Fibber. We will help you. We gave Mr. Shepherd our word.

Reader Leader 3: The villagers ran with Will. They ran all the way to the field. They were very tired.

Reader Leader 1: They were tired, but they gave Mr. Shepherd their word. They would not let him down.

Reader Leader 2: They finally got to the field. They saw the sheep dog. They saw the sheep. They did *not* see Sneaky Wolf!

Reader Leader 3: The villagers looked at Will.

The Villagers: What is going on? We see sheep. We see a sheep dog. But we do NOT see Sneaky Wolf!

Will Fibber: Ha! Ha! Ha! I tricked you! Ha, ha, ha, ha, ha!

The Villagers: This is not funny, Will Fibber. You fibbed to us. You made us leave our work. You made us run to the field. We are tired. This is not funny!

Fables & Folklore Reader's Theater © 2004 Creative Teaching Press

CRYING WOLF

Reader Leader 1: But Will thought it was funny. He thought it was very funny.

Will Fibber: It is not so boring now! Ha, ha, ha, ha, ha!

Reader Leader 2: Days passed. Mr. Shepherd was still on his trip. Will was still in the field.

Will Fibber: It is boring again! So . . . I will play my trick again!

Reader Leader 3: Will ran to the village. He cried "Sneaky Wolf!" again.

Reader Leader 1: Again the villagers left their work. Again the villagers ran to the field to help.

Reader Leader 2: Again they were tired. And again there was no Sneaky Wolf!

The Villagers: This is not funny, Will Fibber. You fibbed to us again. You made us leave our work again. You made us run to the field again. We are tired again. This is not funny! We will not help you again!

Reader Leader 3: Days passed. Mr. Shepherd was still on his trip.

Reader Leader 1: But it was not boring today. No, not today. Out of the woods came Sneaky Wolf.

Reader Leader 2: He hid under a bush in the field. Then he jumped on a sheep.

Fables & Folklore Reader's Theater © 2004 Creative Teaching Press

Will Fibber: OH, NO! OH, NO! Sneaky Wolf IS real! Sneaky Wolf is here. Sneaky Wolf will steal the sheep. I must run to the village.

Reader Leader 3:   Will Fibber ran to the village. He cried:

Will Fibber: Help! Sneaky Wolf! Sneaky Wolf! I need help! Sneaky Wolf is in the field. Please, help me!

The Villagers: We do not believe you, Will. You are a fibber. This time we will not leave our work. This time we will not run to the field. This time we will not help.

Will Fibber: But you gave your word!

The Villagers: Yes! We gave our word to Mr. Shepherd. But this time, you will not trick us again!

Reader Leader 1:   Will ran back to the field alone. Sneaky Wolf had stolen many sheep.

Reader Leader 2:   Will Fibber did not know what to do. But he did know who to blame!

Fables & Folklore Reader's Theater © 2004 Creative Teaching Press

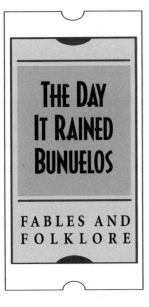

THE DAY IT RAINED BUNUELOS

FABLES AND FOLKLORE

SCRIPT SUMMARY

The Day It Rained Bunuelos is based on a Puerto Rican "Noodlehead Tale." Set the stage by asking children to think about clowns and their job. Clowns try to make people laugh. For many years, people have made up and told clown-like stories about "noodleheads"—people who are easily fooled and/or do silly things. The tales are humorous and meant to entertain—not to be disrespectful! Ask children to relate stories about times when they or their family members have done silly things—like the time Dad couldn't find his glasses and they were on top of his head. Then, introduce these Spanish vocabulary words:

ayyyy: (rhymes with "fry") an expression like "Ohhhhhhh!"

bunuelos: (bun WAY los) deep-fried sweet dessert

casa: (rhymes with "lotsa" without the t) house

mira: (meerah) look

sí: yes

siesta: (see ES tah) a little nap

sombrero: a work hat

tortilla: round flat bread that looks like a pancake but is not sweet

READING REHEARSAL

When you read aloud the script for children, have them listen for the following:

- Some of the words in the story are Spanish not English. Find and pronounce each of the Spanish-language words and expressions for children. Have them repeat the words after you until they are comfortable with each pronunciation. Point out that some members of the audience will not be familiar with the words, and speaking slowly and clearly will help them hear and learn the words.

- Maria likes and takes care of her husband. Her voice should convey this affection. She is amused by his ability to believe anything, but she is not disrespectful. Read aloud her lines to him, modeling a bemused and affectionate tone.

- Three children will read the part of the three robbers together. Have children practice reading in unison.

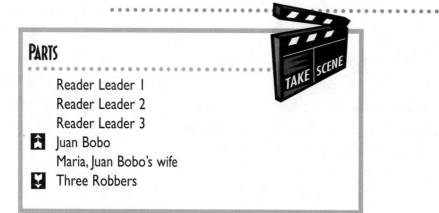

PARTS

Reader Leader 1
Reader Leader 2
Reader Leader 3
Juan Bobo
Maria, Juan Bobo's wife
Three Robbers

DRAMA COACH'S CORNER

Silly Song

OBJECTIVE
Retell key events of the story in a silly song.

ACTIVITY

Give each child a **Silly Story Song reproducible (page 45).** Have children write a silly song about the story. Invite them to sing their silly songs.

Making Bunuelos

OBJECTIVE
Build language experience by making bunuelos.

ACTIVITY

Give each child a **Making Bunuelos reproducible (page 46).** If possible, ask volunteers to bring **ingredients,** and make the bunuelos as a class. Take **photos** as children work and eat the bunuelos. Or, have children take home the recipe and prepare the tasty treat with adult supervision. Afterwards, have children describe the finished product. List their describing words on **chart paper,** and post the list with the photos of the class making and eating bunuelos.

Quick Version: If time is short, you can cut flour tortillas into fourths and fry them in oil instead.

Silly Story Song

Directions: Complete the blanks with a descriptive word for the character, his or her name, the action word, the action of the character, and the story title. Sing your "silly story song" to the tune of "The Farmer in the Dell."

The _____ _____ _____.
            what kind?   who did?   what or where?

The _____ _____ _____.
            what kind?   who did?   what or where?

Ho, ho for _____, **oh!**
                                 Story Title

The _____ _____ _____.
            what kind?   who did?   what or where?

Name_____ Date _____

Making Bunuelos

Directions: Find an adult to help you make this simple recipe. Read and answer the questions after you cook your tasty treat.

Recipe for Bunuelos

Makes 16 servings

Ingredients

4 eggs

¼ cup white sugar

1 tsp vegetable oil

2 cups flour (divided)

1 tsp baking powder

1 tsp salt

1 cup vegetable oil for frying

1 cup white sugar

1 tsp ground cinnamon

Directions

1. Combine eggs and sugar and beat until thick. Add oil.

2. In a new bowl, combine 1½ cups flour, the baking soda, and salt. Mix. Gradually add this to the egg mixture and beat well.

3. Use the remaining flour on the table. Turn the dough onto the floured table and knead until the dough is smooth.

4. Divide the dough into 16 balls. Roll each into a 5" (12 cm) circle. Let the dough sit on waxed paper for 10 minutes.

5. Heat the oil in a deep-fry pan to 350°F (175°C). Fry the circles until golden brown, turning once. Drain them on paper towels. Mix the cinnamon and sugar and sprinkle it on the bunuelos.

What was fun about making the bunuelos? _____

_____

How did the bunuelos taste?_____

_____

Fables & Folklore Reader's Theater © 2004 Creative Teaching Press

THE DAY IT RAINED BUNUELOS

Retold and adapted by Margaret Allen

PARTS

Reader Leader 1
Reader Leader 2
Reader Leader 3
Juan Bobo
Maria, Juan Bobo's wife
Three Robbers

Reader Leader 1: There once was a poor farmer.

Reader Leader 2: He was so honest and trusting. He was easily fooled.

Reader Leader 3: He was called Juan Bobo by all the people in town. That means Juan the Fool in Spanish.

Reader Leader 1: That's not very nice!

Reader Leader 2: No, it is not very nice. But that is what the people called him. This is one of his stories.

Juan Bobo: I am so tired. I am glad I am finally on my way home.

Reader Leader 3: The fields were very hot that day. And Juan Bobo had worked very hard.

Juan Bobo: Maybe I will sit under this tree for a little siesta. Then I will take the long walk back to my casa.

Reader Leader 1: And with that, Juan Bobo sat down under the tree. He propped his head up against the tree trunk. He covered his eyes with his sombrero.

Reader Leader 2: Meanwhile, back at the casa, Maria was looking out of the window. She was getting worried.

Maria: Where is Juan Bobo? The tortillas and beans are getting cold. Where, oh where is that man?

Reader Leader 3: Juan Bobo slept for a long time. When he woke up, he saw three bags hidden between two trees.

Juan Bobo: What is this? Should I open these bags? Sí, I think I should know what is in them.

Reader Leader 1: Juan Bobo was not prepared for what was inside.

Juan Bobo: Ayyyyyyy! Gold! Three bags of gold! I must hurry home to show Maria.

Reader Leader 2: Juan Bobo ran home. He was not tired anymore.

Maria: There you are, Juan Bobo. I was worried. Where have you been?

Juan Bobo: Mira! Look! Gold! Three bags of gold!

Maria: Ayyyyyyy, Juan! That gold must belong to robbers! Do not tell anyone we have it! I will hide the bags.

Reader Leader 3: But Maria knew Juan Bobo was not good at keeping secrets. She must do something. So, she came up with a plan.

Fables & Folklore Reader's Theater © 2004 Creative Teaching Press

THE DAY IT RAINED BUNUELOS

Maria: Juan Bobo, go to town. Bring back eggs, butter, cornmeal, and milk—lots of each!

Juan Bobo: Ay. I am so tired, Maria! But, sí, I will go.

Reader Leader 1: He came home with everything. Then he went right to sleep.

Reader Leader 2: Maria went right to work. She cooked and cooked and cooked.

Reader Leader 3: She made so many bunuelos, the pile touched the ceiling. She took them outside and threw them all over the ground.

Reader Leader 1: The next morning, Juan Bobo got up. He looked out of the window. He could not believe his eyes.

Juan Bobo: Maria, Maria! Mira! Look!

Maria: Ayyyyyyy! It must have rained bunuelos last night!

Reader Leader 2: While Juan Bobo looked at the ground and then the sky, Maria went to the stable.

Reader Leader 3: The donkey was eating a pile of hay. Maria turned the donkey so its tail faced the hay.

Reader Leader 1: Just then, Juan Bobo walked in the stable. He heard his wife say:

THE DAY IT RAINED BUNUELOS

Maria: Ayyyyyyy! It is a miracle, a miracle! The donkey has been eating with its tail!

Reader Leader 2: Poor Juan Bobo. He was so trusting. He believed it rained bunuelos. He believed the donkey ate with its tail.

Reader Leader 3: Juan Bobo was not good with a secret. He told the people in town about the gold. He told the people in town about the bunuelos. And, he told them about the donkey.

Reader Leader 1: The people laughed and laughed. Poor Juan Bobo, they said. Such a fool!

Reader Leader 2: A week later, the three robbers came back to town. They went to the two trees where they had hidden the gold.

Three Robbers: Where is our gold? It is not here! Who took it? Let's go to town and find out.

Reader Leader 3: They went to town. They asked the people about the gold. The robbers looked mean.

Reader Leader 1: So the people in town told them Juan Bobo had the gold. The robbers walked to Juan Bobo's house.

Fables & Folklore Reader's Theater © 2004 Creative Teaching Press

THE DAY IT RAINED BUNUELOS

Three Robbers: Juan Bobo! Is Juan Bobo here? We know you have our gold. Give it back or we will hurt you!

Juan Bobo: Sí, I have the bags. Maria, bring out the gold you hid.

Maria: I do not remember anything about gold.

Juan Bobo: Sure you do. Remember? I gave you the gold. Then I went to sleep. Remember, Maria?

Maria: Gold, Juan Bobo?

Juan Bobo: Sí, Maria, gold! Remember? Then it rained bunuelos. Then the donkey ate with his tail. Don't you remember, Maria?

Reader Leader 2: The three robbers looked at each other. The three robbers looked at Maria.

Reader Leader 3: They looked at Juan Bobo and shook their heads.

Three Robbers: Poor, poor, Juan Bobo. Poor man.

Reader Leader 1: The robbers turned and left. They felt sorry for Maria.

Three Robbers: Oh, that poor woman. What a thing to have married such a fool!

Reader Leader 2: So, from that day on, Juan Bobo and Maria had a very nice life! And no one ever laughed at them again!

Fables & Folklore Reader's Theater © 2004 Creative Teaching Press

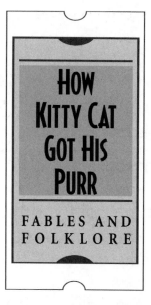

HOW KITTY CAT GOT HIS PURR

FABLES AND
FOLKLORE

SCRIPT SUMMARY

How Kitty Cat Got His Purr is based on a pourquoi (why) tale from the West Indies. Set the stage by asking children if they know why dogs bark or cats purr. Have they ever thought about it before? Some pourquoi tales are passed down by word of mouth in hopes of explaining things in nature. Have children pair off and discuss why they think a cat purrs.

READING REHEARSAL

When you read aloud the script for children, have them listen for the following:

- The story is in rhyme. Point out that students need to be careful not to overemphasize the rhymes with their voice. Demonstrate this by reading a few lines and landing hard on the rhyme or pausing slightly before each rhyming word. Point out that such a reading makes it hard for the listeners to enjoy and hear the story behind the rhyme. Read the same lines again smoothly and with an even modulation.

- The story includes onomatopoeia, or words that describe the sound they represent. List examples such as *woof, bark, drip,* and *bang.* Have children practice making the drum and purring noises.

PARTS

Reader Leader 1   Kitty Cat
Reader Leader 2   Ratty Rat
Reader Leader 3   Uncle Tom Cat

DRAMA COACH'S CORNER

Pourquoi Tale

> OBJECTIVE
> Use the pourquoi story structure to write an original tale.

ACTIVITY

Give each child a **How the Duck Got His Quack reproducible (page 54).** Invite children to make up their own tale to explain why or how something works in nature. Discuss their ideas as a class. Then, have children invent an explanation for how the duck got its quack. Have them draw pictures and present their tale orally. Encourage children to share their story with a partner.

Thinking about Conflict

> OBJECTIVE
> Recall and respond to a scene from the story.

ACTIVITY

Give each child a **Kitty Cat and Ratty Rat reproducible (page 55).** Have children draw a picture in the box to show what turned the two characters from friends to enemies. Then, have children discuss whether or not Kitty Cat should have been angry with Ratty Rat. Ask them to answer the question at the bottom of the page.

Name_____   Date _____

How the Duck Got His Quack
A Pourquoi Tale in Pictures

Directions: Draw pictures to tell your story.

Fables & Folklore Reader's Theater © 2004 Creative Teaching Press

Name_____

Kitty Cat and Ratty Rat

Directions: Kitty Cat and Ratty Rat once were friends. Draw a picture in the box to show what turned them from friends to enemies. Then answer the question at the bottom of the page.

Do you think Kitty Cat should have gotten mad at Ratty Rat? Explain.

_____

_____

_____

_____

How Kitty Cat Got His Purr

Retold and adapted by Margaret Allen

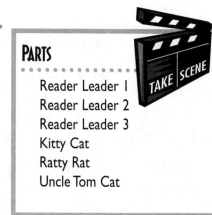

PARTS

Reader Leader 1
Reader Leader 2
Reader Leader 3
Kitty Cat
Ratty Rat
Uncle Tom Cat

Reader Leader 1: Kitty Cat and Ratty Rat once were friends, did you know that?

Reader Leader 2: No! I didn't. Please do tell. Tell it fast. Tell it well.

Reader Leader 3: I will tell you. I'll tell it fast. Of how these friends just did not last.

Reader Leader 1: This is their story—oh, friends of fur. But only Cat ends up with purrrrrrr!

Kitty Cat: Oh, Ratty Rat, I wove mats. A mat for me and a mat for you, Ratty Rat, my good friend true.

Ratty Rat: Oh, Kitty Cat, I made hats. A hat for me and a hat for you, Kitty Cat, my good friend true.

Reader Leader 2: And that's how it was with these friends true. All Kitty Cat had, Ratty Rat had, too.

Reader Leader 3: That is, until Uncle Tom's visit, some will say. It seems things really changed that day.

Uncle Tom Cat: Kitty Cat, Kitty Cat, are you in? Open the door. I want to tell you where I've been!

Fables & Folklore Reader's Theater © 2004 Creative Teaching Press

Kitty Cat: Oh, Uncle Tom Cat, come in. Come in. Please do tell me where you've been.

Uncle Tom Cat: I went to see your Grandpa Cat down in Kittydum. He sent you a little present. See? The cat family drum.

Kitty Cat: Oh, Uncle Tom Cat. That gift is just great. Will you teach me to play it? I can hardly wait!

Uncle Tom Cat: Oh, yes, and with great pleasure. I'll teach you to play. But three things you must know. Three things I must say.

Kitty Cat: Three things, Uncle? Three things to know? Hurry, Uncle! Don't be slow!

Uncle Tom Cat: You must never poke it. Don't beat it. Never rap. Only stroke it gently. You'll take care of it like that.

Kitty Cat: I will not poke it, Uncle. I will never beat or rap. I'll stroke it gently, uh-hum, uh-hum. Now let me play this little drum.

Reader Leader 1: And the sound went purr-ummmm, purr-ummmm.

Reader Leader 2: And then another sound—it was a knock upon the door.

Reader Leader 3: It was Ratty Rat, the friend. He was ready to play some more.

Ratty Rat: Oh, Kitty Cat, my friend true. Where have you been? I've been looking for you!

Kitty Cat: Oh, Uncle, may I show him? May he play my new drum, too? After all, he is my best friend, Ratty Rat, friend so true.

Uncle Tom Cat: I am very sorry. But Grandpa Cat did say only a cat may stroke the drum. Only a cat can play.

Reader Leader 1: And with that, Uncle Tom Cat left the drum and went away.

Reader Leader 2: But, while Kitty Cat said good-bye to Uncle that fine day . . .

Reader Leader 3: . . . Ratty Rat snatched the little drum and he did try to play.

Ratty Rat: If I play Kitty's drum, he will not care. He knows that true friends always like to share.

Reader Leader 1: Ratty Rat tried to poke it. He beat it, then tried to rap.

Reader Leader 2: Then by chance he stroked it as he held it in his lap.

Ratty Rat: Listen to the sound. The sound of the little drum. All I did was stroke it And now? Purr-ummmm! Purr-ummmm!

Fables & Folklore Reader's Theater © 2004 Creative Teaching Press

How Kitty Cat Got His Purr

Kitty Cat: What is that I hear as I come in my own door? Is that you, Ratty Rat, with my new drum on the floor?

Reader Leader 3: Ratty Rat saw his friend. But he didn't look at him the same way!

Reader Leader 1: Why, Kitty Cat looked mad! Like he could *eat* Ratty Rat today!

Reader Leader 2: And so Ratty Rat ran fast, and Kitty Cat ran fast, too.

Reader Leader 3: Kitty Cat opened wide—aaaah, hummmmm! But all he swallowed was the little drum!

Kitty Cat: And ever since that day, I have my drum with me. But not that rascal Ratty Rat—he is now my enemy!

Reader Leader 1: And now Kitty Cat always knows who plays his tiny drum.

Reader Leader 2: Remember, if you are kind to the cat, he may purr-ummmm for you! Uh-hum!

Reader Leader 3: But do not poke at Kitty Cat. Never beat him and never rap.

Reader Leader 1: Just stroke Kitty Cat gently—listen now. Do you hear it? Do you hear purr-ummmm, purr-ummmm?

Reader Leader 2: For when you hear the purring, that's Kitty Cat's little drum!

Fables & Folklore Reader's Theater © 2004 Creative Teaching Press

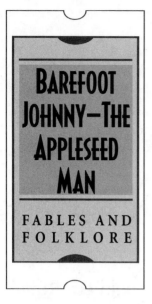

BAREFOOT JOHNNY—THE APPLESEED MAN

FABLES AND FOLKLORE

Script Summary

Barefoot Johnny—The Appleseed Man is based on the folk legend (and tall tale) of pioneer John Chapman who wandered barefoot through the wilderness of the Midwest. In this Reader's Theater version, he and his brother, Nathaniel (Nat), part company so Johnny can begin his mission. Set the stage for reading by asking children if they like apples. Ask how many ways they have had apples prepared. Then, introduce the story.

Reading Rehearsal

When you read aloud the script for children, have them listen for the following:

- Johnny is worried that Nat will be disappointed in his idea in the beginning. Model reading his lines in a worried tone. Read Nat's lines in a reassuring manner. Have children mimic your reading.

- Write Johnny's part on the board when he calls for people to come and get his seeds. Note that this part must be read with a strong clear voice or the people he called to would not hear or understand him. Have all children practice reading that part from the board.

PARTS

Reader Leader 1	Child 1
Reader Leader 2	Child 2
Johnny	Child 3
Nat	Child 4

DRAMA COACH'S CORNER

Thematic Literature Share

OBJECTIVE
Write a poem about Johnny Appleseed's experience.

ACTIVITY

Give each child a **Back in Time with Johnny Appleseed reproducible (page 62).** Read to the class other **stories about Johnny** such as these:

• *Johnny Appleseed* by Reeve Lindbergh (Little, Brown and Company)

• *Johnny Appleseed* by Steven Kellogg (Morrow Junior Books)

• *The Story of Johnny Appleseed* by Aliki (Prentice-Hall)

Have children close their eyes for guided visualization as you help them to mentally see, hear, smell, touch, and taste the wilderness Johnny covered barefoot, pot on head, in ragged clothes as he distributed his apple seeds. Then, have children write a five senses poem about Johnny's wilderness.

Apple Products

OBJECTIVE
Group themed illustrations.

ACTIVITY

Give each child an **Apple Collage reproducible (page 63)** and **grocery store ads, catalogs, magazines,** and **food labels.** Have children create an apple product collage on their reproducible.

Back in Time with Johnny Appleseed

Directions: Think about the story of Johnny Appleseed. Where does it take place? Draw a picture of the story setting in the box. Write a poem about what you would see, hear, smell, taste, feel, and know about if you could go back in time with Johnny Appleseed.

I see _____

I hear _____

I smell _____

I taste _____

I feel _____

I know _____

Apple Collage

Directions: Cut out pictures of items made from apples and glue them in the space below to create an apple collage.

BAREFOOT JOHNNY—THE APPLESEED MAN
Retold and adapted by Margaret Allen

PARTS

Reader Leader 1
Reader Leader 2
Johnny
Nat
Child 1
Child 2
Child 3
Child 4

Reader Leader 1: Do you like apples?

Reader Leader 2: Yes, I do! And applesauce, apple pie, apple juice, apple . . .

Reader Leader 1: Okay! Okay! I get it. You like apples!

Reader Leader 2: You DID ask me, you know! But why?

Reader Leader 1: Because I just heard a great story about apples. A story about apples and the man who planted them. Want to hear it?

Reader Leader 2: Yes, I do.

Reader Leader 1: The story begins with Johnny and his brother Nat. They were planning a big trip.

Johnny: Nat, oh, Nat. Please come here. I have something to tell you.

Nat: What is it, Johnny? I am busy packing for our trip.

Johnny: That's what I want to talk to you about. I am not going with you. I can't.

Nat: What? Not going? But we had a plan!

Fables & Folklore Reader's Theater © 2004 Creative Teaching Press

Johnny: I know. But I have a new plan now.

Nat: What is your new plan, Johnny?

Johnny: I am going to take a trip. A great big trip all over this country.

Nat: I know! Our trip! Our trip will be all over this country!

Johnny: No, not our trip. My trip. Nat, I must do this my way. I plan to take apple seeds to every farmer.

Nat: Apple seeds? What are you talking about?

Johnny: Nat, you know that I love apples. The farmers and their kids will love them, too. So I will bring seeds to them. But, I need your help.

Nat: My help? With what?

Johnny: Please fill all of these bags with seeds. Then, put these bags in the canoe.

Nat: Are you sure about this, Johnny?

Johnny: You bet I am. This is my new job. I will give apple seeds to everyone I meet. I will plant apple trees every place I go. Soon this country will have apples everywhere!

Nat: Everywhere, Johnny? Okay, if you say so!

Fables & Folklore Reader's Theater © 2004 Creative Teaching Press

Johnny: Thank you for your help. Good-bye, Nat.

Nat: Good-bye, Johnny. And, good luck!

Reader Leader 2: Nat watched his brother Johnny leave. He watched him paddle away in the canoe.

Reader Leader 1: Nat knew his brother had a dream—an apple dream. Nat knew his brother wanted to help people.

Reader Leader 2: Nat knew that his brother was special!

Reader Leader 1: Johnny paddled his canoe. He paddled a long time. Then he saw farmers. He called from his canoe.

Johnny: Seeds! Seeds! Apple seeds! Come and get your free apple seeds!

Reader Leader 2: Where Johnny could not go by canoe, he walked. As he walked near towns, he called:

Johnny: Seeds! Seeds! Apple seeds! Come and get your free apple seeds!

Reader Leader 1: And people came. They planted the apple seeds.

Reader Leader 2: The apples grew and grew. All over the country, apples grew.

Reader Leader 1: People began to know Johnny. Farmers knew him. Townspeople knew him.

Fables & Folklore Reader's Theater © 2004 Creative Teaching Press

Reader Leader 2: And children knew him. When he came into town, they called.

All Children: Hi, Johnny! Hi, Johnny Appleseed. Thank you for the seeds. Thank you for my apple trees.

Reader Leader 1: As Johnny walked away, the children talked about him. They told each other stories they had heard.

Child 1: Johnny Appleseed does not have a compass. But he never gets lost!

Child 2: Johnny Appleseed does not have any shoes. But even in the snow, his feet never get cold.

Child 3: Johnny Appleseed does not have a hat. But he wears a pot on his head instead.

Child 4: Johnny Appleseed does not have a family. But kids everywhere love him.

Reader Leader 2: Yes, people all over this country knew Johnny. People all over this country loved Johnny—Johnny Appleseed, as they called him.

Child 1, 2, 3, 4: Thank you, Johnny Appleseed. Thank you for the seeds. Thank you for my apple trees. Thank you for being so special!

Fables & Folklore Reader's Theater © 2004 Creative Teaching Press

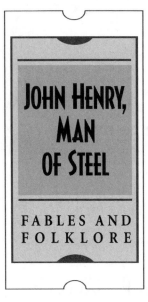

JOHN HENRY, MAN OF STEEL

FABLES AND FOLKLORE

SCRIPT SUMMARY

John Henry, Man of Steel is based on the song and story of the American tall tale figure, John Henry. Bring in books about trains, pictures of railroads, or train and tunnel models to set the stage for reading the story. Talk about the objects depicted. Introduce the words *steel rails, railroad ties, steel spikes, steel driving man,* and *steam drill.* Show pictures of each from the books or artifacts presented earlier. Explain that this tall tale is from an earlier time in America's history and that the main
character of the story is a folk hero.

READING REHEARSAL

Copy the script onto overhead transparencies, and display them. When you read aloud the script for children, have them listen for the following:

• Discuss the pride Mama and Daddy Henry had when their son was born.

• Display the third page of the script and talk about Polly Ann's *worry* for her husband. Read her parts together.

• Call attention to the last page when the story moves from complete joy at John Henry's victory to sadness as he is worn out.

PARTS

Reader Leader 1   Mama Henry
Reader Leader 2   John Henry
Reader Leader 3   Polly Ann
Daddy Henry

DRAMA COACH'S CORNER

Fatherly Advice

OBJECTIVE
Internalize and express the message of the story.

ACTIVITY

Give each child an **I Did It! reproducible (page 70)**. Have children discuss the advice John Henry's father gave him to always do his best. Invite children to talk about a time they tried something hard, did their best, and felt good about the results.

Superhero

OBJECTIVE
Relate characteristics of a character to self.

ACTIVITY

Give each child a **Superhero reproducible (page 71)**. Explain to children that John Henry is a folk legend, a tall tale figure, or, in other words, a superhero. Ask children to pretend they are superheroes. How would they dress? What would they do? What "super-props" would they need? Invite children to respond on the reproducible.

I Did It!

Directions: Write about a time you tried something hard and did it.

One time, when I was ____ years old, I tried to _____

_____

_____

_____

_____

_____

_____

_____

_____

_____

_____

And I did it!

Fables & Folklore Reader's Theater © 2004 Creative Teaching Press

Name_____ Date _____

Superhero

Directions: Pretend you are a superhero. What is your name? Draw a picture showing how you look, what you do, and what "super-prop" you will use.

Name:

John Henry, Man of Steel

Retold and adapted by Margaret Allen

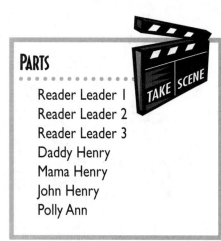

Parts

Reader Leader 1
Reader Leader 2
Reader Leader 3
Daddy Henry
Mama Henry
John Henry
Polly Ann

Reader Leader 1: It was a cold, black night. The moon was red. Lightning flashed. Thunder rolled.

Reader Leader 2: And at midnight, John Henry was born. Born with a hammer in his hand!

Daddy Henry: Mama, we have a real man now. Do you see that hammer in his hand?

Mama Henry: Yes, I do. This boy will grow up to be very strong. This boy will grow up to be very special!

Reader Leader 3: John Henry was big for a baby. He learned to crawl very soon. He crawled with his hammer.

Daddy Henry: John Henry, my boy, you crawl with your hammer. It's okay. You will grow up to be strong.

Mama Henry: John Henry, use your hammer. It's okay. You will grow up to be special!

Fables & Folklore Reader's Theater © 2004 Creative Teaching Press

JOHN HENRY, MAN OF STEEL

Reader Leader 1: "Bang! Bang!" sounded the hammer in the day. "Bang! Bang!" went the hammer in the night.

Reader Leader 2: At four, John Henry was getting big. At four, he was big enough to do chores.

Daddy Henry: John Henry, whatever you do, do it right. John Henry, whatever you do, do it well.

Mama Henry: That's right. Listen to your daddy.

Daddy Henry: Always be a real man. Always do your best, son.

Reader Leader 3: John Henry grew up. He left home with his hammer. He left to find a job. But he would never forget what his daddy and mama told him!

Reader Leader 1: John Henry saw men laying a new railroad.

John Henry: That might be the job for me. I can carry heavy steel rails. I can lay them on the railroad ties. I can hammer the steel spikes into the ties. I can!

Reader Leader 2: The railroad crew boss hired John Henry. He had never seen such a huge, strong man before.

Reader Leader 3: So, John Henry became a steel driving man. People all over the land heard about John Henry. That's because he was the best.

Fables & Folklore Reader's Theater © 2004 Creative Teaching Press

Reader Leader 1: Polly Ann heard about him, too. She went to the railroad tracks to find him.

Reader Leader 2: John Henry saw Polly Ann. She had a sweet face. John Henry liked her right away.

John Henry: Polly Ann, will you marry me?

Polly Ann: Yes! You are very strong. But you are also nice. You work hard. You do your best. I will always be proud of you.

Reader Leader 3: John Henry and Polly Ann married. They were very happy.

Reader Leader 1: One day, the head of the railroad went to see John Henry. He went to offer him a new job.

Reader Leader 2: The man told John Henry they were building a new railroad track. And the longest railroad tunnel ever made—right through a mountain! The railroad wanted John Henry to be their steel driving man.

John Henry: What do you think, Polly Ann? They want me! They want me for their steel driving man.

Polly Ann: But, John Henry, I have been to that mountain. It is the biggest mountain I have ever seen.

Fables & Folklore Reader's Theater © 2004 Creative Teaching Press

John Henry: Don't worry, Polly Ann. You know me. You know all I want to do is hammer all day long. You know I want to be the best steel driving man in the land.

Polly Ann: Then you better take the job, John Henry. But be safe! And don't work too hard!

Reader Leader 3: John Henry took the job. He started working on the tunnel through the mountain.

Reader Leader 1: One day, there was a huge blast. The tunnel caved in. John Henry used his hammer to save a crew of trapped men. He was a hero!

Reader Leader 2: The word spread fast. Everyone knew about John Henry—that there was nothing he couldn't do!

Reader Leader 3: Another railroad company heard about John Henry. They wanted to test him. They had a steam drill that could do more work than sixteen men, they said.

Reader Leader 1: John Henry can beat that thing, his men said.

Reader Leader 2: So a contest was set—John Henry against the steam drill.

Polly Ann: Remember what I said, John Henry. Do not work too hard. You will wear yourself out!

Fables & Folklore Reader's Theater © 2004 Creative Teaching Press

John Henry: And you remember what I said, Polly Ann. A man's got to be a real man. A man has to do his best. If that means I will wear out, then I will wear out! I am the best steel driving man. I will win.

Reader Leader 3: And so it was—John Henry against the steam drill. At first, John Henry did well. He was winning. Then the steam drill started to win.

Reader Leader 1: First, John Henry worked with one hammer. Then he worked with two hammers. He worked and he worked.

Polly Ann: John Henry, you won! Yay! You won! But stop now. You are wearing out!

Reader Leader 2: Yes, John Henry won. He heard the cheers. He also heard Polly Ann. But he didn't stop. He hammered and hammered until he finished the tunnel all by himself!

Reader Leader 3: Then John Henry looked at Polly Ann. She rushed over to him. He was tired. He was more than tired!

Polly Ann: Oh, John Henry! I told you not to work so hard. You have worn yourself out!

John Henry: Yes, I think I did this time. Take me home. I cannot work anymore. But, when I die, make sure you tell everyone about me. Tell them I was a steel driving man—the best steel driving man in the land!

Reader Leader 1: And so the story goes that even though John Henry is gone, you can still hear his hammer singing.

Reader Leader 2: Every time you hear a train rolling across the country, listen! It is the song of John Henry, the best steel driving man in the land!

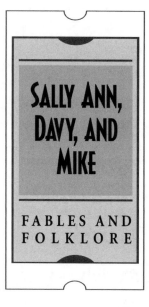

SALLY ANN, DAVY, AND MIKE

FABLES AND FOLKLORE

SCRIPT SUMMARY

Sally Ann, Davy, and Mike is based on three American tall tale figures: Davy Crockett, his legendary wife Sally Ann Thunder Ann Whirlwind, and riverboat man Mike Fink. Name each of the three folk heroes, and ask children if they have ever heard about them. What do they know? Discuss their responses, and then introduce the story.

READING REHEARSAL

When you read aloud the script for children, have them listen for the following:

- Point out that the script contains some language used in casual conversation in some parts of the country. Have children identify some of these words such as *howdy, yep,* and *nope.*

- Explain that the tall tale calls for a spirited and highly modulated reading. Exaggerate the "larger than life" characters through your reading, and have small groups of volunteers mimic you.

- Point out that Sally Ann Thunder Ann Whirlwind Crockett's name is a play on words. If they same the name quickly, they'll hear that the *Ann* is meant to stand for the word *and.* The name implies that Sally was loud like thunder and wild like a whirlwind. Crockett was her married name.

PARTS

Reader Leader 1
Reader Leader 2
Reader Leader 3
⭐ Sally Ann Thunder Ann Whirlwind Crockett
⭐ Davy Crockett
⭐ Mike Fink

DRAMA COACH'S CORNER

Retell It!

> **OBJECTIVE**
> Retell the story using character cutouts.

ACTIVITY

Give each child a **Sally Ann, Davy, and Mike reproducible (page 80), craft sticks,** and **glue.** Have children cut out and color the characters and glue each onto a craft stick. Then, have them retell the story for a partner or the class.

Comparison Poem

> **OBJECTIVE**
> Write a comparison poem about a tall tale character.

ACTIVITY

Give each child a **Tall Tale Characters reproducible (page 81).** Have children write a comparison poem about one of the characters in the story: Davy Crockett, Mike Fink, or Sally Ann.

Tall Tale Characters

As brave as any man,
As tall as a tree,
As loud as a siren,
Is Sally.

Name_____   Date _____

Sally Ann, Davy, and Mike

Directions: Color and cut out the characters. Glue each one to a craft stick to make a puppet. Use your puppets to retell the story.

Name_____ Date _____

Tall Tale Characters

Directions: Choose a tall tale character from the story. Draw the character in the center of the box. Think of three words to describe the character and write them in the first blank of lines one, two, and three. Write three other things that fit the one-word description in the second blank of lines one, two, and three. Write the character's name in the last blank.

As _____ as _____,

As _____ as _____,

As _____ as _____,

Is _____.

SALLY ANN, DAVY, AND MIKE

Retold and adapted by Margaret Allen

PARTS

Reader Leader 1
Reader Leader 2
Reader Leader 3
Sally Ann Thunder Ann
 Whirlwind Crockett
Davy Crockett
Mike Fink

Davy Crockett: Howdy, folks! Did you ever hear the tale of a mighty gal? Her name was Sally Ann Thunder Ann Whirlwind Crockett.

Reader Leader 1: I don't think so.

Davy Crockett: Well, she was amazing! She was as tall as a tree. And folks say she always carried a big sack of rattlesnakes with her.

Reader Leader 2: Wasn't she scared of snakes?

Davy Crockett: Nope! She wasn't scared of anything. She was very brave. And . . . she was my wife.

Reader Leader 3: Your wife?

Davy Crockett: Yep! My wife. Want to hear a story about her?

Reader Leader 1: Yes! I want to hear it. We have read all about you. But we never read about your wife, Sally Ann.

Fables & Folklore Reader's Theater © 2004 Creative Teaching Press

SALLY ANN, DAVY, AND MIKE

Davy Crockett: I know! That's what most folks say. But I'm gonna change all that . . . right now! I'm gonna ask Mike Fink to help me tell her story. Okay with you, Mike?

Mike Fink: Shucks, Davy. You know I hate that story. You just want me to tell it 'cause Sally Ann got the better of me! That's all!

Davy Crockett: Of course! Why else?

Mike Fink: This is how it happened. Davy and I were always fighting. We were rivals, you might say.

Sally Ann: You *might* say? Hey, boys. Don't I get to help spin this yarn? It is my story, too, you know.

Mike Fink: Oh, howdy, Sally Ann. I didn't know you were in these parts. Sure—join in. You may as well!

Reader Leader 2: Oh, please tell us your story, Sally Ann. We would love to hear it from you!

Sally Ann: Thanks, darlin'. My name is Sally Ann. But folks all over called me Sally Ann Thunder Ann Whirlwind— that is, until I met Davy.

Davy Crockett: I fell for her right away. Soon, we got hitched.

Fables & Folklore Reader's Theater © 2004 Creative Teaching Press

Sally Ann: That's right! Then folks stuck Crockett at the end. Sally Ann Thunder Ann Whirlwind Crockett! That's my full name!

Reader Leader 3: That is a very long name!

Sally Ann: As I was saying, I got picked on a lot! See, most folks didn't like my bonnet, you know, my hat.

Reader Leader 1: Your hat? Why didn't they like your hat?

Mike Fink: It was a beehive, I tell you! She wore a beehive for a bonnet!

Sally Ann: As I was saying, I wore a bearskin for a dress. Folks didn't like that either. I guess it was 'cause I skinned that bear myself.

Davy Crockett: That's right! She could skin a bear fast. Faster than an alligator could eat a fish!

Mike Fink: Yea, and she could holler louder than a mountain lion—I should know!

Sally Ann: I could also take care of myself! Like the day Mike Fink over there tried to scare me.

Mike Fink: I knew this was coming—you just have to tell that story, don't you?

Fables & Folklore Reader's Theater © 2004 Creative Teaching Press

Sally Ann: Yes, I do, Mike. I am not one to brag, but you asked for it.

Davy Crockett: Mike told folks he was gonna scare Sally Ann. He said he would scare her so much her teeth would rattle!

Sally Ann: He dressed up like a critter.

Mike Fink: Yea, I reckon I did. I dressed up in an alligator skin. I got down on all fours. Then I waited.

Reader Leader 2: Don't even tell me how you got an alligator skin!

Davy Crockett: Mike waited and waited for Sally Ann. Then he saw her. She was out taking her nightly walk.

Mike Fink: I crawled over to her. I got up close. I pushed her with my alligator head.

Davy Crockett: That's when most gals would have been scared. But not my wife . . . not my Sally Ann!

Mike Fink: Then I stood up and tried to hug her!

Reader Leader 3: Oh, no! What did you do then, Sally Ann? Weren't you scared? I would have been!

Sally Ann: Why, I got mad! I said to that critter—that's it! No critter hugs me and gets away with it.

Sally Ann, Davy, and Mike

Mike Fink: Then she let out a holler that could hurt your ears!

Davy Crockett: Yep! Then she walloped him so hard *his* teeth rattled!

Mike Fink: They still do.

Sally Ann: Only when you brag too much, Mike Fink! And we all know how much *you* like to brag!

Mike Fink: Yep! But now I have to think twice about it!

Davy Crockett: You see, most folks *do* hear his teeth rattle when he brags! You know what I mean?

Reader Leader 1: Wow! That's an amazin' . . . I mean, amazing story!

Reader Leader 2: Thank you, Sally Ann, Davy, and Mike.

Reader Leader 3: Yes! Thanks for sharing such a wild tale with us!

Davy Crockett: Why, shucks! Nothing to it! I was glad to do it!

Fables & Folklore Reader's Theater © 2004 Creative Teaching Press

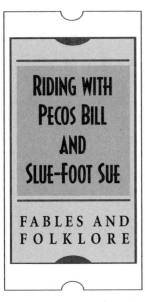

RIDING WITH PECOS BILL AND SLUE-FOOT SUE

FABLES AND FOLKLORE

SCRIPT SUMMARY

Riding with Pecos Bill and Slue-Foot Sue is based on the American tall tale characters Pecos Bill and his sweetie, Slue-Foot Sue. Ask children to describe a Texas cowboy. What would he wear? Look like? Do? Now multiply that ten times, and you have a tall tale Texas cowboy named Pecos Bill. Think of a girl who could match his greatness, and you have Slue-Foot Sue. Use this discussion to introduce the story. You might also wish to define the following words for children:

bronco:	a male horse, still untamed, used for rodeo events
corral:	a fenced in area for horses
coyote:	a small canine, close cousin to wolves or wild dogs, common in the southern half of the United States
howdy:	hi
pardners:	partners, or someone with whom you are friendly
slue-foot:	to move unpredictably
smitten:	in love
steel-spring bustle:	a fashion accessory that fit under a woman's skirt to make it seem more full in the back, no longer in use

READING REHEARSAL

When you read aloud the script for children, have them listen for the following:

- Remind children that since this is such a tall tale, their voices should be greatly exaggerated.

- The characters speak in colloquial language and often use unfamiliar words or drop the endings of their words.

- Call attention to the differences in loud Pecos Bill's voice, slow-talking Cowpoke Cody's voice, and sneaky Widow Maker's voice. Slue-Foot Sue is almost as loud and outspoken as Pecos Bill. Select one part from each of the characters, and model it. Have children echo-read with expression just as you modeled.

PARTS

Reader Leader 1   Pecos Bill

Reader Leader 2   Widow Maker

☘ Cowpoke Cody   ☘ Slue-Foot Sue

DRAMA COACH'S CORNER

Widow Maker

OBJECTIVE
Describe a character from the story.

ACTIVITY

Give each child a **Character Poem reproducible (page 89)**. Discuss with children
Widow Maker's character. Why did he behave the way he did? Have children write a
shape poem about Widow Maker's character. Invite children to share their completed
poems with the class.

Literature Response

OBJECTIVE
Recall and visualize a scene from the story.

ACTIVITY

Give each child a **Pecos Bill reproducible (page 90)**. Have children draw their favorite
part of the story. Since this is an oral story without much visual support, children will
have to demonstrate story comprehension to visualize the characters and setting. Invite
children to share their completed drawings.

Character Poem

Directions: To create a shape poem, think of three descriptive words or phrases about Widow Maker's character. Write them on the lines provided. On the last line, rename Widow Maker.

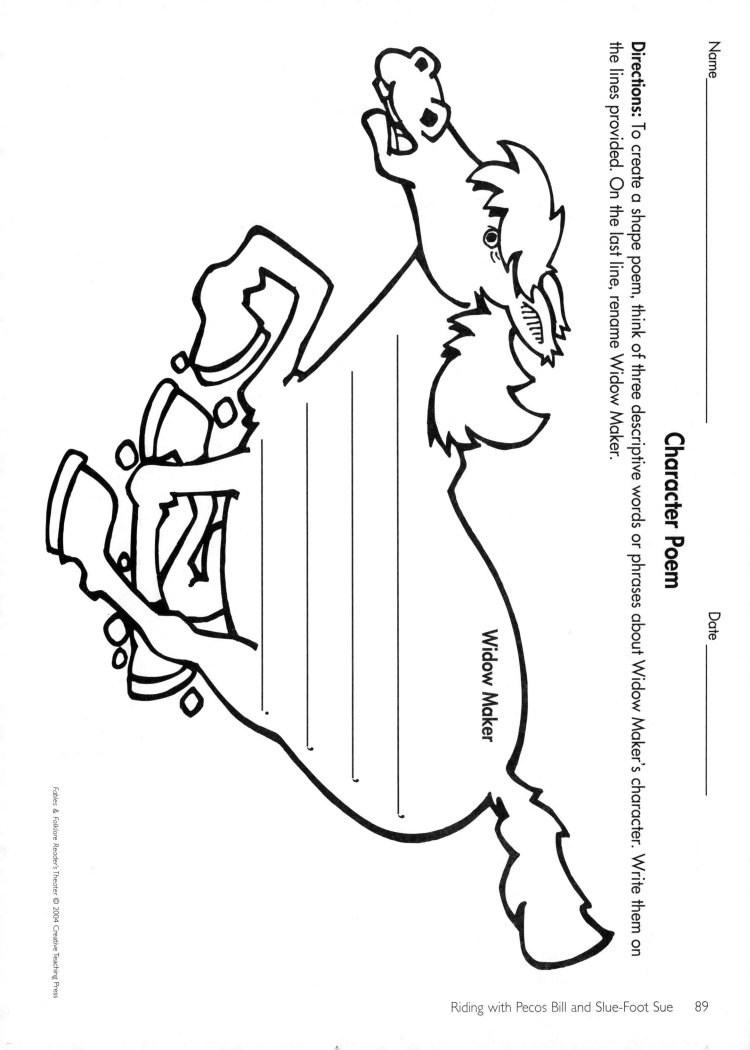

Widow Maker

Name_____ Date _____

Pecos Bill

Directions: Draw a scene from your favorite part of the story about Pecos Bill.

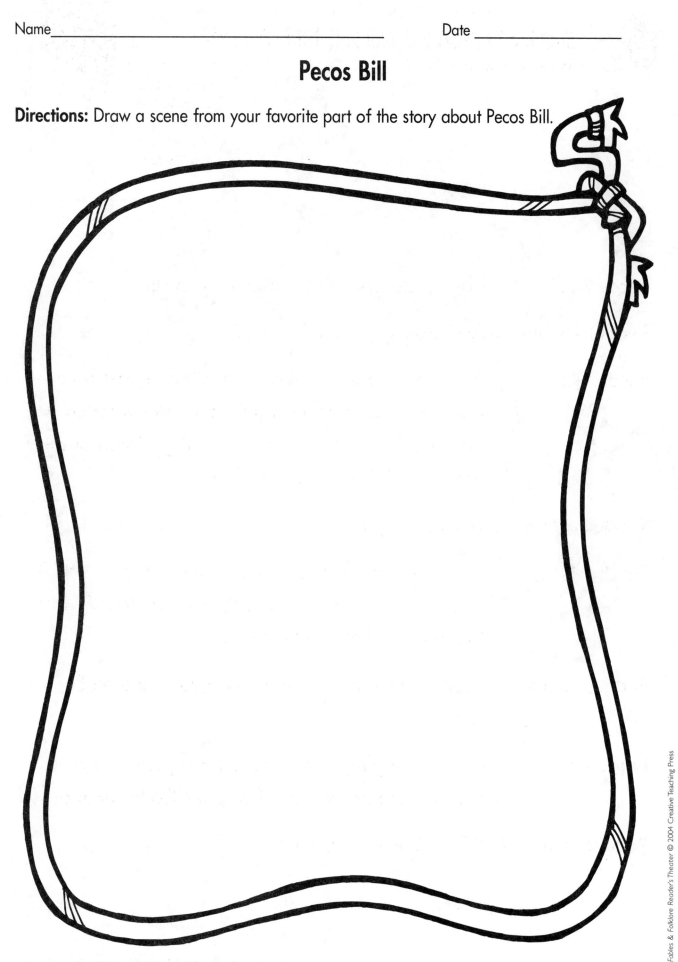

Fables & Folklore Reader's Theater © 2004 Creative Teaching Press

RIDING WITH PECOS BILL AND SLUE-FOOT SUE

Retold and adapted by Margaret Allen

Pecos Bill: Howdy, pardners! My name is Pecos Bill.

Reader Leader 1: And, howdy to you, Pecos Bill.

Pecos Bill: This is my story. You see, I was born in east Texas. I had fourteen brothers and sisters. We went on a long trip. When they started fighting—I was pushed right out of the wagon!

Reader Leader 2: Where did you land?

Pecos Bill: I fell out in west Texas, land of the coyotes. Why, it was the coyotes that raised me. I guess that's why I've always been a little bit wild!

Reader Leader 1: That's not what I heard. I heard you were really wild!

Pecos Bill: As I was saying, I was raised by coyotes. I was happy. But then one day Cowpoke Cody came by.

Reader Leader 2: Who's Cowpoke Cody?

Pecos Bill: He was a cowboy—and a right friendly guy. He saw me on the ground—you know, with the coyotes?

Cowpoke Cody: Pecos Bill, what are you doing on the ground? Why you're acting like a coyote. Don't you know you are a man? Now get up and act like one!

Pecos Bill: I guess I did think I was a coyote. I sure could holler and howl like one—ah-hoooooo!

Cowpoke Cody: Now wash up. Put on these clothes. I'm taking you to town—and to people! No more living like a coyote!

Reader Leader 1: So, Pecos Bill, did you go to live in town?

Pecos Bill: Yes, I did. And, that's where I met Widow Maker.

Widow Maker: Neighhhhhh! That's me! I met Pecos Bill and Cowpoke Cody the first day they came to town.

Pecos Bill: That's right! I never saw a horse buck so much!

Widow Maker: That's what I like to do—buck! Why, I was bucking off cowpoke after cowpoke. Then Cowpoke Cody walked over to the corral. He talked to Pecos Bill.

Cowpoke Cody: Watch it, Pecos Bill. Step aside. I'm gonna ride that wild bronco. And I'm gonna ride him now. Help me up.

Widow Maker: He only thought he was gonna ride me. I bucked him off on his head. His brain is still rattling around in there!

Pecos Bill: I helped Cowpoke Cody up. I took him out of the corral. Folks came over to take care of him.

Reader Leader 1: Then what did you do, Bill?

Pecos Bill: I turned to Widow Maker. I said, "Widow Maker, you wild bronco, now it's my turn!"

Widow Maker: I don't know why, but I liked Bill right off the bat. So I bucked a bit, and then I let him ride me.

Pecos Bill: Yea, I rode him. And I liked that wild horse. From then on, Widow Maker and I were always together.

Widow Maker: That is, until one day, when something awful happened!

Slue-Foot Sue: Howdy! I guess that's where I come into the story. I met Pecos Bill just after he got to town. I think he was smitten with me. And I sure was with him!

Pecos Bill: Sure enough! The first time I saw Slue-Foot Sue, her long red hair was blowing in the wind. And, she was riding on the back of the biggest catfish I ever did see!

Reader Leader 2: Is that true, Sue? You rode a catfish?

Fables & Folklore Reader's Theater © 2004 Creative Teaching Press

Slue-Foot Sue: I reckon so. Why, I was having fun! All the folks in town said I was a bit wild 'cause I was riding that catfish and all. I didn't care much what they said. I was having fun!

Widow Maker: I could see right away that I was in trouble. Bill took to Sue like a fish to water. I could see she would come between us, so I didn't like her much.

Reader Leader 1: I guess Pecos Bill fell in love with Slue-Foot Sue.

Reader Leader 2: Yes, and I bet he asked her to marry him. Did you, Pecos Bill? Did you ask her to marry you?

Pecos Bill: I sure did! Sue said she would marry me, but only if I let her ride Widow Maker!

Reader Leader 1: Oh, Sue! You wanted to ride that wild horse? That sounds like a big mistake to me!

Widow Maker: You are right. It was a mistake. It was a mistake for her! Sue showed up for the wedding in a pretty white dress.

Pecos Bill: She was prettier than anything I had ever seen!

Reader Leader 2: Did her dress have a steel-spring bustle in the back? I read that was the style then.

Fables & Folklore Reader's Theater © 2004 Creative Teaching Press

RIDING WITH PECOS BILL AND SLUE-FOOT SUE

Widow Maker: It sure did have a bustle! Big mistake for Sue!

Slue-Foot Sue: Pecos Bill showed up in his fancy buckskin suit. He looked mighty handsome on our wedding day.

Pecos Bill: Thanks, darling. As soon as we were hitched, Sue said . . .

Slue-Foot Sue: . . . Okay, Pecos Bill. I am your wife. Now do I get to ride that wild bronco of yours?

Pecos Bill: I feel real uneasy about that, Sue. But I said you could, so you can. I keep my word!

Widow Maker: I couldn't wait! Sue got on my back in that fancy dress of hers. I started bucking and bucking. She went higher and higher—with that bustle!

Pecos Bill: Stop that, Widow Maker! Stop!

Widow Maker: But I didn't stop! That bustle of hers was like a giant spring. She kept right on springing higher and higher. Soon, she was going up into the clouds.

Pecos Bill: Sue, I'll save you. I'll save you, darlin'. I'll lasso you and bring you down. Ready? Grab the rope.

Slue-Foot Sue: I've got it, Bill. Help me.

Pecos Bill: Oh, no, Sue! I'm going up with you. Good-bye, Widow Maker. Good-bye, everyone!

Widow Maker: It looks like they are flying to the moon!

Reader Leader 2: To the moon? Are you sure?

Widow Maker: Nope! But I don't think any of us will ever see Pecos Bill and Slue-Foot Sue again!

Fables & Folklore Reader's Theater © 2004 Creative Teaching Press